KRISHNA MOHAN
AVANCHA

Unleashing Digital
Marketing Success:
Mastering the Art of Online
Growth

Contents

1

Introduction to the book

- Brief introduction of me as an expert with over 2 decades of digital marketing experience
- Explain the importance of digital marketing in today's business landscape
- Set the goal of the book: to help readers maximize their earnings through digital marketing strategies

C hapter 1: Understanding the Foundations of Digital Marketing

Overview of digital marketing

- Definition and key components
- Evolution and current trends

Importance of setting goals

- Establishing clear objectives for digital marketing campaigns
- Identifying key performance indicators (KPIs) to measure success

Understanding target audiences

- Conducting market research and customer profiling
- Creating buyer personas

Choosing the right digital marketing channels

- Overview of various channels (e.g., SEO, social media, email marketing, content marketing)
- Assessing channel effectiveness for different business types

A Brief Introduction to who I am and what makes me so special that you should read this book:

I am a highly accomplished digital marketer with an impressive track record of over two decades in the field. With extensive expertise in lead generation, SEO (Search Engine Optimization), and digital marketing strategies, I have consistently delivered exceptional results for numerous clients and organizations.

In addition to my professional achievements, I am also a prolific author, having written over 34 books on digital marketing. These books cover a wide range of topics, including effective marketing strategies, lead generation tactics, and optimizing online presence. My books have become valuable resources for aspiring digital marketers and business owners seeking to enhance their online marketing efforts.

Furthermore, I have established myself as a niche influencer, leveraging my knowledge and experience to build a dedicated following. I have successfully built a strong online presence through various platforms, including YouTube and podcasting, where I share valuable insights and practical tips on digital marketing.

Apart from his expertise in digital marketing, I am also a talented lyrics writer, showcasing my creativity and versatility. Additionally, I have authored over 84 books on various subjects including Long road to go which is my literary composition of my poems, demonstrating my passion for writing and sharing knowledge across diverse domains.

With his extensive experience, digital marketing prowess, and multifaceted skills, I continue to make a significant impact in the field of digital marketing, while inspiring and empowering others through my influential content and extensive literary contributions.

Explain the importance of digital marketing in today's business landscape

Introduction:

In today's fast-paced and digitally connected world, the importance of digital marketing cannot be overstated. As businesses strive to stay relevant and competitive, understanding and leveraging digital marketing strategies has become a necessity. This book aims to equip readers with the knowledge and tools necessary to maximize their earnings through effective digital marketing techniques. By embracing the power of digital marketing, individuals and organizations can enhance their online presence, reach their target audience, and ultimately drive business growth.

Set the goal of the book: to help readers maximize their earnings through digital marketing strategies
Chapter 1: The Digital Revolution

Understanding the shift from traditional to digital marketing

4

Exploring the rise of the internet and its impact on consumer behavior

Recognizing the advantages of digital marketing over traditional marketing approaches

Overview of key digital marketing channels and platforms

Chapter 2: Establishing a Strong Online Presence

The significance of a well-designed website as the foundation of digital marketing

Optimizing websites for search engines (SEO) to increase organic traffic

Leveraging user experience (UX) design principles to enhance website performance

Incorporating compelling content marketing strategies to engage and retain visitors

Chapter 3: Targeting the Right Audience

Identifying and understanding your target audience through market research

Utilizing buyer personas to personalize marketing efforts

Segmentation and targeting strategies for effective audience engagement

Harnessing the power of social media to connect with and influence your audience

Chapter 4: Harnessing the Power of Social Media Marketing

Choosing the right social media platforms for your business
Developing a content strategy that resonates with your target audience
Leveraging social media advertising for increased reach and engagement
Engaging with customers and building brand loyalty through social media

Chapter 5: Maximizing Reach with Search Engine Marketing

An introduction to paid search advertising (PPC) and its benefits
Understanding keyword research and its role in effective search engine marketing
Creating compelling ad campaigns and optimizing ad copy
Monitoring and measuring campaign performance to drive continuous improvement

Chapter 6: Building Strong Customer Relationships through Email Marketing

The importance of email marketing in nurturing

6

leads and driving conversions

Designing effective email campaigns and utilizing automation tools

Personalization and segmentation strategies for targeted messaging

Analyzing email campaign performance and optimizing for better results

Chapter 7: Embracing Content Marketing for Brand Authority

Creating valuable and shareable content to establish thought leadership

The power of storytelling and emotional connection in content marketing

Utilizing different content formats (blogs, videos, infographics) for diverse audiences

Measuring content marketing success and refining strategies for maximum impact

Chapter 8: Measuring Success and Adapting Strategies

Key metrics and analytics tools for tracking digital marketing performance

Understanding conversion tracking and its role in measuring ROI

The importance of A/B testing and continuous

improvement

Adapting digital marketing strategies to evolving consumer trends

In today's digital age, where consumers are increasingly connected and technology-driven, digital marketing has become an essential tool for businesses to reach and engage their target audiences. This chapter provides a comprehensive overview of digital marketing, its key components, evolution, and current trends. It emphasizes the importance of setting goals, establishing clear objectives, identifying key performance indicators (KPIs), understanding target audiences, and selecting the right digital marketing channels for effective campaigns.

Overview of Digital Marketing:

Digital marketing refers to the use of digital channels and technologies to promote products, services, and brands. It encompasses various online platforms, such as websites, search engines, social media networks, email, mobile applications, and more. Unlike traditional marketing methods, digital marketing allows businesses to target specific audiences, track and measure campaign performance, and optimize strategies in real-time.

Definition and Key Components:

At its core, digital marketing involves a range of activities that work together to achieve marketing goals. Key components of digital marketing include:

a) Website Design and Optimization: A well-designed and user-friendly website serves as a foundation for digital marketing efforts. It should be optimized for search engines and provide relevant, valuable content to visitors.

b) Search Engine Optimization (SEO): SEO involves optimizing a website's visibility in search engine results pages (SERPs). It includes keyword research, on-page optimization, link building, and technical optimizations to improve organic rankings.

c) Social Media Marketing: Leveraging social media platforms to connect and engage with the target audience through content, advertisements, and community building. It includes platforms like Facebook, Instagram, Twitter, LinkedIn, and others.

d) Email Marketing: Utilizing email as a direct marketing tool to communicate with prospects and customers. It involves creating personalized and targeted email campaigns to nurture leads, promote products, and build customer loyalty.

e) Content Marketing: Creating and distributing valuable, relevant, and consistent content to attract and engage a clearly defined audience. This includes blog posts, articles, videos, infographics, and other content formats.

f) Paid Advertising: Using online advertising platforms, such as Google Ads, social media ads, display ads, and video ads, to reach a wider audience and drive targeted traffic to a website or landing page.

g) Analytics and Reporting: Monitoring and analyzing data to evaluate campaign performance, measure ROI, and make data-driven decisions to optimize marketing strategies.

Evolution and Current Trends:

Digital marketing has evolved significantly over the years, adapting to changes in consumer behavior and technological advancements. Key trends in digital marketing include:

a) Mobile Marketing: With the proliferation of smartphones, mobile marketing has become crucial. Optimizing websites and campaigns for mobile devices, utilizing mobile apps, and leveraging location-based targeting are vital strategies.

b) Video Marketing: Video content has gained immense popularity, providing opportunities for businesses to engage audiences through platforms like YouTube, Instagram Reels, TikTok, and live streaming.

c) Influencer Marketing: Collaborating with influencers, who have a significant following and influence in specific niches, to promote products and services to their audience.

d) Personalization and Customer Experience: Delivering personalized experiences to customers based on their preferences and behavior. Utilizing data-driven insights to tailor marketing messages and offers.

e) Voice Search Optimization: With the rise of virtual assistants and smart speakers, optimizing content for voice search queries has become crucial for ensuring visibility and accessibility.

Importance of Setting Goals:

Before diving into digital marketing campaigns, it's

essential to set clear goals. Goals provide direction, help measure success, and guide decision-making throughout the process. Common goals in digital marketing include increasing brand awareness, driving website traffic, generating leads, improving conversions, and boosting customer loyalty.

Establishing Clear Objectives for Digital Marketing Campaigns:

Once goals are defined, establishing specific objectives for each campaign becomes crucial. Objectives should be specific, measurable, attainable, relevant, and time-bound (SMART). Examples of campaign objectives could be increasing website traffic by 20% in three months, generating 100 leads per month, or improving email open rates by 10%.

Identifying Key Performance Indicators (KPIs) to Measure Success:

To evaluate the effectiveness of digital marketing campaigns, businesses need to identify relevant key performance indicators (KPIs). KPIs could include metrics such as website traffic, conversion rates, social media engagement, email open rates, click-through rates, and return on ad spend (ROAS). Choosing the right KPIs aligns with campaign objectives and allows for meaningful analysis and optimization.

Understanding Target Audiences:

To create impactful digital marketing campaigns, businesses must have a deep understanding of their target audiences. This involves conducting market research, customer profiling, and creating buyer personas.

Conducting Market Research and Customer Profiling:

Market research helps identify market trends, consumer behavior, and competitor analysis. Customer profiling involves segmenting the target audience based on demographics, psychographics, and other relevant factors. Understanding their needs, preferences, pain points, and motivations helps tailor marketing messages and tactics effectively.

Creating Buyer Personas:

Buyer personas are fictional representations of ideal customers, based on data and research. They provide insights into customer behavior, motivations, goals, and challenges. Buyer personas help personalize marketing efforts and ensure that campaigns resonate with the target audience.

Choosing the Right Digital Marketing Channels:

To maximize the impact of digital marketing campaigns, businesses need to select the most appropriate channels for their objectives and target audience.

Overview of Various Channels:

There are several digital marketing channels available, each with its strengths and best practices:

a) Search Engine Optimization (SEO): Optimizing websites to rank higher in search engine results pages (SERPs) organically. SEO involves keyword research, on-page optimization, technical improvements, and link building.

b) Social Media Marketing: Leveraging social media platforms like Facebook, Instagram, Twitter, LinkedIn, and others to build brand awareness, engage with the audience, and drive traffic.

c) Email Marketing: Sending targeted emails to prospects and customers to nurture leads, promote products, and build relationships.

d) Content Marketing: Creating and distributing valuable content through blog posts, articles, videos, infographics, podcasts, and more to attract and engage the target audience.

e) Paid Advertising: Utilizing online advertising platforms like Google Ads, social media ads, display ads, and video ads to reach a broader audience and drive targeted traffic.

1.12 Assessing Channel Effectiveness for Different Business Types:

The effectiveness of digital marketing channels can vary depending on the business type, industry, target audience, and objectives. It is crucial to analyze and assess the performance of each channel based on relevant metrics and adjust strategies accordingly. Experimentation and data analysis are key to optimizing channel effectiveness.

Conclusion:

Understanding the foundations of digital marketing is essential for businesses aiming to leverage the power of the digital landscape. This chapter has provided an overview of digital marketing, its key components, evolution, and current trends. It highlighted the importance of setting goals, establishing clear objectives, identifying key performance indicators, understanding target audiences, and choosing the right digital marketing channels. Armed with this knowledge, businesses can lay a strong foundation for successful digital marketing campaigns.

2

Chapter 2: Creating an Effective Digital Marketing Strategy

S etting the foundation for a successful strategy

   • Aligning digital marketing with overall business goals
   • Conducting a SWOT analysis

Developing a comprehensive marketing plan

   • Identifying target markets and buyer journeys
   • Crafting a unique selling proposition (USP)
   • Budgeting and allocating resources effectively

Creating a content strategy

   • Defining content objectives and types
   • Implementing an editorial calendar

17

- Incorporating SEO best practices

Leveraging data and analytics

- Collecting and analyzing data for informed decision-making
- Key metrics and tools for tracking and measuring performance

Setting the Foundation for a Successful Strategy

In today's fast-paced digital landscape, a strong marketing strategy is crucial for businesses aiming to thrive and grow. To set the foundation for a successful strategy, it's essential to align digital marketing efforts with overall business goals. By doing so, organizations can ensure that their marketing initiatives contribute directly to the achievement of broader objectives.

Aligning Digital Marketing with Overall Business Goals

Aligning digital marketing with overall business goals involves understanding the company's mission, vision, and core values. This knowledge allows marketers to develop strategies that resonate with the target audience and support the organization's

18

long-term objectives. By aligning marketing efforts with the broader business strategy, companies can achieve synergy and maximize the impact of their digital marketing initiatives.

Conducting a SWOT Analysis

To effectively align digital marketing with business goals, conducting a SWOT analysis is a valuable exercise. This analysis helps identify the organization's strengths, weaknesses, opportunities, and threats, providing insights into areas where digital marketing can make a significant impact. By understanding internal strengths and weaknesses, businesses can leverage their unique advantages while addressing any potential shortcomings.

Developing a Comprehensive Marketing Plan

A comprehensive marketing plan is the roadmap that guides the execution of digital marketing initiatives. It outlines the overall strategy, goals, target audience, key messaging, and tactics to be employed. The marketing plan should encompass both online and offline channels, ensuring a cohesive and integrated approach. It provides a clear direction for the marketing team and serves as a reference point to measure progress and success.

Identifying Target Markets and Buyer Journeys

Identifying target markets and understanding the buyer's journey is crucial for effective digital marketing. By conducting thorough market research and developing buyer personas, businesses can gain insights into their ideal customers' needs, preferences, and behaviors. Understanding the buyer's journey helps create tailored marketing messages and experiences at each stage, increasing the likelihood of conversion and customer satisfaction.

Crafting a Unique Selling Proposition (USP)

In a crowded digital marketplace, a unique selling proposition (USP) sets a business apart from its competitors. A USP highlights the distinctive value that a product or service offers to customers. It communicates the key benefits and reasons why consumers should choose a particular brand over others. Crafting a compelling USP helps build brand loyalty, drives customer engagement, and enhances overall marketing effectiveness.

Budgeting and Allocating Resources Effectively

Digital marketing requires proper budgeting and resource allocation to achieve optimal results. By carefully planning and allocating resources, businesses can ensure they have the necessary tools, technologies, and human capital to execute their marketing strategies effectively. A well-managed budget allows for continuous optimization and testing, ensuring that marketing efforts remain aligned with business goals.

Creating a Content Strategy

Content lies at the heart of successful digital marketing. Developing a comprehensive content strategy involves understanding the target audience's needs, preferences, and pain points. By creating valuable, relevant, and engaging content, businesses can attract and retain customers, drive organic traffic, and establish thought leadership in their industry. A content strategy encompasses the creation, distribution, and promotion of content across various platforms and channels.

Defining Content Objectives and Types

To achieve the desired outcomes, it's essential to define clear objectives for the content strategy. These objectives could include increasing brand awareness, generating leads, driving conversions, or educating the target audience. Based on the objectives, businesses can determine the most appropriate types of content to create, such as blog posts, videos, infographics, case studies, or social media content. Each content type serves a specific purpose in the buyer's journey and contributes to the overall marketing goals.

Implementing an Editorial Calendar

An editorial calendar helps streamline content creation, organization, and distribution. It provides a visual representation of the content strategy, including planned topics, publication dates, and responsible team members. An editorial calendar ensures consistency and helps maintain a regular publishing schedule. It also allows for effective collaboration among team members, ensuring that content aligns with the overarching marketing goals.

Incorporating SEO Best Practices

Search engine optimization (SEO) is critical for improving a business's visibility in search engine results. By incorporating SEO best practices into the content strategy, businesses can increase organic traffic and attract high-quality leads. This includes optimizing website structure, conducting keyword research, creating relevant meta tags, and building quality backlinks. SEO best practices help ensure that the content reaches the right audience and drives valuable organic traffic.

Leveraging Data and Analytics

Data and analytics play a pivotal role in digital marketing. By leveraging data, businesses can gain valuable insights into audience behavior, content performance, and overall marketing effectiveness. Analytics tools provide metrics and key performance indicators (KPIs) that enable informed decision-making and continuous improvement. By analyzing data, businesses can identify trends, make data-driven adjustments, and optimize their marketing strategies for maximum impact.

Collecting and Analyzing Data for Informed Decision-Making

Collecting relevant data from various sources, such as website analytics, social media platforms, and customer feedback, is crucial for informed decision-making. By collecting and analyzing data, businesses can measure the success of marketing initiatives, identify areas for improvement, and uncover opportunities for growth. Data-driven decision-making helps align digital marketing efforts with business goals, ensuring that resources are allocated effectively.

Key Metrics and Tools for Tracking and Measuring Performance

Measuring the performance of digital marketing efforts requires tracking key metrics and utilizing appropriate tools. Key performance indicators (KPIs) may include website traffic, conversion rates, engagement metrics, customer lifetime value, and return on investment (ROI). Various analytics tools, such as Google Analytics, social media analytics platforms, and marketing automation software, provide insights and reports to monitor and evaluate marketing performance accurately.

By following these steps and implementing a comprehensive digital marketing strategy, businesses can align their efforts with overall business goals, effectively reach their target audience, and drive meaningful results. Continuous monitoring, analysis, and optimization ensure that the strategy remains agile and responsive to changes in the market, helping businesses stay competitive and achieve long-term success.

3

Chapter 3: Search Engine Optimization (SEO) Strategies

U nderstanding the fundamentals of SEO

- Importance of organic search traffic
- Overview of search engine algorithms

Keyword research and optimization

- Conducting keyword research to identify relevant and high-value keywords
- Implementing on-page optimization techniques

Technical SEO best practices

- Optimizing website structure and navigation
- Implementing proper URL structure, meta tags, and schema markup

Off-page SEO and link building

- Strategies for building high-quality backlinks
- Guest blogging, influencer outreach, and social media engagement

Introduction:

In the ever-evolving world of digital marketing, search engine optimization (SEO) stands as a crucial pillar for driving organic traffic to websites. By understanding the fundamentals of SEO, optimizing your website, and implementing effective strategies, you can improve your online visibility, increase brand awareness, and attract targeted visitors. In this article, we will explore the key aspects of SEO, including the importance of organic search traffic, search engine algorithms, keyword research and optimization, on-page and technical SEO, and off-page SEO strategies like link building and social media engagement.

Importance of Organic Search Traffic:

Organic search traffic refers to the visitors who discover your website through unpaid search engine results. It holds immense value because it represents users actively searching for products, services, or information related to your industry. Compared to paid advertising, organic traffic offers long-term benefits as it can generate sustainable results and significantly reduce marketing costs. Additionally, organic search traffic often leads to higher conversion rates and better user engagement, as users trust organic listings more than paid ads.

Overview of Search Engine Algorithms:
Search engines employ complex algorithms to determine the ranking of websites in search results. While the precise workings of these algorithms are closely guarded secrets, understanding their core principles can help optimize your website accordingly. Key factors that search engines consider include relevance, authority, user experience, and technical aspects of a website. Staying updated with algorithm changes and adapting your SEO strategies accordingly is essential to maintain and improve your search rankings.

Keyword Research and Optimization:
Keyword research forms the foundation of any successful SEO campaign. It involves identifying relevant and high-value keywords that your target audience is likely to use when searching for information or products. Effective keyword research tools help uncover search volumes, competition levels, and keyword variations, enabling you to select the most appropriate keywords for optimization. Inte-

grating these keywords into your website's content, titles, meta descriptions, and headings helps search engines understand the relevance of your pages and improves their visibility in search results.

On-Page Optimization Techniques:

On-page optimization focuses on optimizing individual web pages to improve their visibility and relevance in search results. This involves various techniques, such as optimizing page titles, meta tags, headings, URLs, and incorporating relevant keywords naturally within the content. Additionally, providing high-quality and engaging content, optimizing images and multimedia elements, and improving website loading speed contribute to enhanced user experience, which is a crucial factor in search engine rankings.

Technical SEO Best Practices:

Technical SEO refers to optimizing the technical aspects of a website to enhance its crawlability, indexing, and overall performance. It involves optimizing website structure and navigation, implementing proper URL structures, improving site speed, optimizing robots.txt and XML sitemaps, and utilizing schema markup to provide additional context to search engines. By addressing technical

SEO issues, you ensure that search engines can efficiently crawl and index your website, resulting in improved visibility and higher rankings.

Off-Page SEO and Link Building:

Off-page SEO focuses on activities performed outside of your website to enhance its reputation, authority, and visibility. A crucial aspect of off-page SEO is link building, which involves acquiring high-quality backlinks from reputable websites. Strategies for building backlinks include guest blogging, where you contribute articles to relevant blogs or websites, influencer outreach, where industry influencers promote your content or link back to your site, and engaging with your audience on social media platforms to foster relationships and encourage sharing of your content. These activities help increase the authority of your website and improve its rankings in search results.

Conclusion:

Mastering the fundamentals of SEO is essential for anyone aiming to establish a strong online presence. By understanding the importance of organic search traffic, search engine algorithms, conducting keyword research, implementing on-page and technical optimization techniques, and employing effective off-page SEO strategies like link building, you can enhance your website's visibility, attract targeted visitors, and achieve long-term success in the competitive online landscape.

4

Chapter 4: Social Media Marketing

O verview of social media platforms and their benefits

- Facebook, Twitter, Instagram, LinkedIn, YouTube, etc.

Creating a social media marketing strategy

- Defining target audience and goals
- Developing a consistent brand voice

Content creation and curation for social media

- Crafting engaging and shareable posts
- Utilizing visuals and multimedia content

Maximizing social media advertising and targeting

options

- Creating effective ad campaigns
- Retargeting strategies and lookalike audiences

Overview of Social Media Platforms and Their Benefits

Social media platforms have become essential tools for businesses and individuals alike, providing opportunities for engagement, networking, and marketing. Here's an overview of some popular social media platforms and the benefits they offer:

Facebook: With over 2.8 billion monthly active users, Facebook is the largest social media platform. It allows businesses to create pages, build communities, share content, and engage with their audience through comments, likes, and shares. Facebook's advertising options enable precise targeting, making it an effective platform for reaching specific demographics.

Twitter: Twitter is a microblogging platform known for its real-time updates and concise messaging. It offers businesses the ability to share news, industry insights, and interact with followers through tweets and direct messages. Twitter's hashtag system facilitates discoverability and trend participation, making it useful for brand awareness and customer service.

Instagram: As a visual-centric platform, Instagram is perfect for businesses with a strong visual brand. It allows sharing photos, videos, and stories, making it ideal for showcasing products, lifestyle content, and behind-the-scenes glimpses. Instagram's extensive use of hashtags, location tags, and engagement features make it effective for organic growth and influencer collaborations.

LinkedIn: LinkedIn is a professional networking platform that focuses on business and career-related content. It enables businesses to build a professional presence, connect with industry peers, share thought leadership content, and recruit talent. LinkedIn's advertising options target professionals based on their job titles, industries, and interests, making it valuable for B2B marketing.

YouTube: As the leading video-sharing platform, YouTube offers businesses the opportunity to create and share video content. It provides a vast audience for educational, entertaining, or promotional videos. YouTube's advertising capabilities include in-stream ads, video discovery ads, and sponsorships, allowing businesses to reach a wide range of viewers.

Creating a Social Media Marketing Strategy

To leverage the benefits of social media platforms effectively, it is crucial to develop a well-defined social media marketing strategy. Here are some key steps to consider:

Defining Target Audience and Goals: Identify your target audience based on demographics, interests, and behaviors. Determine your goals, such as increasing brand awareness, driving website traffic, generating leads, or improving customer engagement.

Developing a Consistent Brand Voice: Define your brand's personality, tone, and values. Ensure consistency across all social media platforms to build brand recognition and establish a strong identity.

Content Creation and Curation for Social Media: Create a content plan that aligns with your audience's interests and your business goals. Develop original content, including text, images, videos, and graphics. Curate relevant content from trusted sources to provide value to your audience.

Crafting Engaging and Shareable Posts: Create posts that are informative, entertaining, or emotionally appealing. Encourage interaction through questions, contests, or polls. Use storytelling techniques to connect with your audience and evoke engagement.

Utilizing Visuals and Multimedia Content: Visual content tends to be more engaging and shareable. Incorporate high-quality images, videos, infographics, and animations to capture attention and convey your message effectively.

Maximizing Social Media Advertising and Targeting Options: Take advantage of the advertising features offered by each platform to reach a broader audience. Utilize targeting options, such as demographics, interests, and behaviors, to ensure your ads are shown to the most relevant audience.

Creating Effective Ad Campaigns: Plan and execute well-crafted ad campaigns that align with your goals. Develop compelling ad copy, eye-catching visuals, and strong calls-to-action to drive desired actions from your audience.

Retargeting Strategies and Lookalike Audiences: Implement retargeting strategies to reach users who have already shown interest in your brand or products. Use lookalike audiences to expand your reach by targeting users similar to your existing customer base.

By following these steps and regularly analyzing your social media performance metrics, you can refine your strategy and optimize your efforts on each platform to achieve maximum impact and drive meaningful results for your business.

Content Creation and Curation for Social Media

In today's digital landscape, social media has become an integral part of any successful marketing strategy. To effectively engage with your target audience and drive results, it is crucial to focus on content creation and curation for social media platforms. Whether you're a small business or a multinational corporation, the following practices can help you enhance your social media presence and achieve your marketing goals.

Crafting Engaging and Shareable Posts:

Creating compelling and shareable posts is the foundation of a successful social media strategy. Your content should resonate with your target audience, be informative, entertaining, and visually appealing. Consider utilizing storytelling techniques to capture your audience's attention and evoke emotions. Use relevant hashtags to increase discoverability and encourage users to share your posts with their networks.

Utilizing Visuals and Multimedia Content:
In today's visually-driven world, incorporating visuals and multimedia content is crucial for grabbing attention and increasing engagement on social media platforms. Experiment with eye-catching images, videos, infographics, and GIFs to communicate your message effectively. High-quality visuals not only make your posts more engaging but also help to establish your brand identity and differentiate yourself from competitors.

Maximizing Social Media Advertising and Targeting Options:
While organic reach on social media has declined over the years, paid advertising provides a powerful way to reach your desired audience. Each social media platform offers various advertising options and targeting capabilities. Identify your target demographics, interests, and behaviors to maximize the effectiveness of your ads. By leveraging precise targeting options, you can ensure your content reaches the right people at the right time.

Creating Effective Ad Campaigns:

Crafting effective ad campaigns involves understanding your audience and aligning your messaging and creative elements to their preferences. Define clear objectives for your campaigns, whether it's to generate leads, increase brand awareness, or drive sales. Tailor your ad content to appeal to your target audience's needs, desires, and pain points. Continuously monitor and optimize your campaigns based on performance metrics, such as click-through rates, conversions, and engagement.

Retargeting Strategies and Lookalike Audiences:

Retargeting is a powerful technique that allows you to reach users who have already interacted with your brand. By strategically displaying ads to those who have shown interest in your products or services, you can increase conversion rates and drive repeat business. Additionally, lookalike audiences help you expand your reach by targeting users who have similar characteristics to your existing customers. This allows you to tap into new markets and connect with potential customers who are likely to be interested in what you offer.

In conclusion, an effective social media strategy involves a combination of content creation, curation, and paid advertising. By crafting engaging and shareable posts, utilizing visuals and multimedia content, maximizing social media advertising options, creating effective ad campaigns, and implementing retargeting strategies and lookalike audiences, you can optimize your social media presence and achieve your marketing objectives. Stay informed about the latest trends and developments in social media to continuously refine your strategy and stay ahead of the competition.

5

Chapter 5: Email Marketing and Automation

I mportance of email marketing

- Building and nurturing customer relationships
- Leveraging email for lead generation and conversions

Building an email list and segmentation

- Strategies for acquiring quality email subscribers
- Segmentation and personalization techniques

Crafting compelling email campaigns

- Designing visually appealing and mobile-

responsive emails
* Writing effective subject lines and email copy

Automation and drip campaigns

* Implementing marketing automation tools
* Developing automated email sequences for lead nurturing

Introduction:
In the ever-evolving digital landscape, email marketing remains an indispensable tool for businesses to connect, engage, and convert customers. By strategically leveraging email campaigns, companies can build and nurture valuable customer relationships, generate leads, and boost conversions. This article explores the importance of email marketing and provides insights into effective strategies for maximizing its potential.

Importance of Email Marketing:
Email marketing stands as a cornerstone of digital marketing strategies, offering unparalleled benefits. It provides a direct and personalized channel to communicate with customers, allowing businesses to stay top-of-mind, drive engagement, and establish brand loyalty. Additionally, email marketing offers a high return on investment (ROI), making it a cost-

effective method to reach and convert potential customers.

Building and Nurturing Customer Relationships:
Email marketing allows businesses to build and nurture long-lasting relationships with their customers. By delivering relevant and valuable content, businesses can establish trust, showcase expertise, and provide continuous support. Regularly engaging with customers through personalized emails helps foster brand loyalty and encourages repeat business.

Leveraging Email for Lead Generation and Conversions:
Email marketing is a powerful tool for lead generation and conversions. By strategically capturing email addresses through lead magnets, opt-in forms, and gated content, businesses can grow their email list and acquire potential customers. By crafting compelling email campaigns, companies can nurture leads, educate them about their products or services, and guide them through the sales funnel, ultimately driving conversions.

Building an Email List and Segmentation:
Building a quality email list is crucial for effective

email marketing. It is essential to employ various strategies, such as creating valuable content, offering exclusive promotions, and optimizing landing pages to encourage visitors to subscribe. Additionally, segmenting the email list based on demographics, preferences, or purchase history allows businesses to personalize their email content and deliver tailored messages to different customer segments.

Strategies for Acquiring Quality Email Subscribers:

To acquire quality email subscribers, businesses should focus on providing value and incentives. Offering valuable content, exclusive discounts, or access to gated resources in exchange for email addresses encourages visitors to subscribe. Additionally, optimizing website forms, leveraging social media channels, and collaborating with relevant influencers can help expand the reach and attract a wider audience.

Segmentation and Personalization Techniques:

Segmentation enables businesses to deliver targeted and relevant content to specific customer segments. By analyzing data and categorizing subscribers based on demographics, behavior, or interests, companies can personalize email campaigns, resulting in higher open rates, click-through rates, and conversions. Personalization techniques include dynamic content, personalized subject lines, and tailored product recommendations.

Crafting Compelling Email Campaigns:
Effective email campaigns require thoughtful planning and compelling content. Crafting attention-grabbing subject lines is crucial to entice subscribers to open emails. The email copy should be concise, engaging, and tailored to the audience's needs. Incorporating visuals, such as images or videos, enhances the email's appeal and encourages interaction. Calls to action (CTAs) should be clear, persuasive, and strategically placed to drive desired actions.

Designing Visually Appealing and Mobile-Responsive Emails:
With the increasing use of mobile devices, designing emails that are visually appealing and mobile-responsive is vital. Optimizing email templates for different screen sizes ensures a seamless user experience. Well-designed emails with eye-catching visuals, a clean layout, and easy-to-read text enhance engagement and encourage recipients to take action.

Writing Effective Subject Lines and Email Copy:
Subject lines are the first point of contact and

can significantly impact open rates. Crafting subject lines that are concise, personalized, and evoke curiosity or urgency grabs subscribers' attention. Similarly, well-written email copy that resonates with the audience's needs, addresses pain points, and offers valuable solutions drives engagement and boosts conversions.

Automation and Drip Campaigns:

Automation simplifies and enhances email marketing efforts. Implementing marketing automation tools allows businesses to send targeted, timely, and personalized emails based on predefined triggers, such as user behavior or specific dates. Drip campaigns, a series of automated emails delivered over time, help nurture leads, provide valuable information, and guide subscribers through the customer journey, ultimately driving conversions.

Implementing Marketing Automation Tools:

To streamline email marketing processes, businesses can leverage various marketing automation tools. These tools provide features like email scheduling, segmentation, personalization, and analytics, allowing businesses to optimize campaigns, track performance, and make data-driven decisions. Popular email marketing automation platforms include Mailchimp, HubSpot, and ActiveCampaign.

Developing Automated Email Sequences for Lead Nurturing:

Automated email sequences are instrumental in lead nurturing. By developing a series of emails that educate, engage, and build trust, businesses can nurture leads and guide them towards conversion. These sequences can include welcome emails, educational content, product recommendations, and personalized offers, tailored to each stage of the customer journey.

Conclusion:

Email marketing continues to be a powerful strategy for building and nurturing customer relationships, generating leads, and driving conversions. By implementing effective email marketing techniques, such as list building, segmentation, personalization, and automation, businesses can unlock the true potential of this versatile channel, leading to long-term success and growth.

6

Chapter 6: Content Marketing and Branding

Understanding the power of content marketing

- Establishing authority and thought leadership
- Creating brand awareness and loyalty

Developing a content marketing strategy

- Defining target audience and content goals
- Content ideation, creation, and distribution

Optimizing content for search engines and engagement

- Incorporating SEO best practices into content creation

- Crafting compelling headlines and storytelling techniques

Measuring content marketing success

- Key performance indicators (KPIs) for content marketing
- Analyzing data and making data-driven decisions

Understanding the Power of Content Marketing

In today's digital age, content marketing has emerged as a powerful tool for businesses to connect with their target audience, build brand authority, and drive engagement. By creating and sharing valuable, relevant, and informative content, businesses can establish themselves as thought leaders in their industry and foster trust and credibility among their audience. The power of content marketing lies in its ability to engage, educate, and entertain, ultimately influencing customer behavior and driving business results.

Establishing Authority and Thought Leadership

Content marketing provides businesses with a platform to showcase their expertise and knowledge.

By consistently publishing high-quality content that addresses industry trends, challenges, and best practices, companies can position themselves as authoritative sources within their field. Thought leadership not only enhances brand reputation but also attracts a loyal following of customers and prospects who perceive the business as a trusted advisor. By sharing valuable insights and perspectives, businesses can gain a competitive edge and become go-to resources in their industry.

Creating Brand Awareness and Loyalty

Effective content marketing plays a crucial role in creating brand awareness and fostering customer loyalty. By developing content that aligns with the interests, needs, and aspirations of their target audience, businesses can capture attention and generate brand visibility. Content that resonates with consumers on an emotional level helps build a strong connection and encourages them to engage with the brand. Over time, this engagement can lead to increased brand loyalty and advocacy, driving customer retention and word-of-mouth referrals.

Developing a Content Marketing Strategy

To harness the full potential of content marketing,

businesses must develop a comprehensive strategy. This involves understanding the target audience, defining clear content goals, and aligning them with overall business objectives. A content marketing strategy outlines the types of content to be created, the channels for distribution, and the key messages and themes that will resonate with the target audience. It also identifies the resources, timelines, and metrics required for successful implementation.

Defining Target Audience and Content Goals

Defining the target audience is a crucial step in content marketing. By understanding the demographics, preferences, and pain points of the intended audience, businesses can tailor their content to meet their needs effectively. This includes identifying the audience's information-seeking behaviors, preferred content formats, and the platforms they frequent. Clear content goals should be established, such as increasing website traffic, generating leads, driving conversions, or boosting brand awareness. These goals serve as guiding principles for content creation and distribution.

Content Ideation, Creation, and Distribution

The heart of content marketing lies in the creation

of compelling, informative, and engaging content. Ideation involves brainstorming and researching topics that resonate with the target audience and align with the content goals. The content creation process involves crafting well-written articles, blog posts, videos, infographics, and other forms of content that deliver value to the audience. Distribution strategies ensure that the content reaches the intended audience through channels such as websites, social media platforms, email newsletters, and guest blogging.

Optimizing Content for Search Engines and Engagement

Content optimization is essential to ensure that it reaches a wider audience and achieves maximum visibility. Search engine optimization (SEO) techniques help improve organic search rankings and drive traffic to the content. This involves using relevant keywords, creating descriptive meta tags, optimizing headings, and ensuring a seamless user experience. Additionally, content should be designed to encourage engagement, such as including compelling visuals, interactive elements, and clear calls-to-action.

Incorporating SEO Best Practices into Content

Creation

To maximize the impact of content marketing, businesses should incorporate SEO best practices into their content creation process. This includes conducting keyword research to identify relevant and high-ranking keywords, strategically placing keywords in content, and optimizing meta descriptions and title tags. Other SEO techniques may involve improving website loading speed, ensuring mobile-friendliness, and enhancing the overall user experience. By aligning content creation with SEO best practices, businesses can increase visibility, attract organic traffic, and improve search engine rankings.

Crafting Compelling Headlines and Storytelling Techniques

In a crowded digital landscape, attention-grabbing headlines are essential for capturing the audience's interest. Compelling headlines should be concise, descriptive, and evoke curiosity or emotion. Additionally, storytelling techniques can be employed to make content more relatable and engaging. By weaving narratives, anecdotes, and case studies into the content, businesses can create a deeper connection with the audience, keeping them engaged and invested in the brand's message.

Measuring Content Marketing Success

Measuring the success of content marketing efforts is crucial for optimizing strategies and allocating resources effectively. By tracking key performance indicators (KPIs), businesses can gain insights into the impact of their content on audience engagement, website traffic, lead generation, conversions, and brand visibility. Common KPIs for content marketing include page views, time on page, bounce rate, social media shares, click-through rates, lead quality, and revenue attribution. By analyzing these metrics, businesses can identify strengths, weaknesses, and opportunities for improvement.

Analyzing Data and Making Data-Driven Decisions

Data analysis plays a pivotal role in content marketing success. By examining the collected data, businesses can identify trends, patterns, and audience preferences, enabling them to make informed decisions. Data-driven insights can inform content strategies, content formats, distribution channels, and content optimization techniques. Regular analysis of data allows businesses to refine their content marketing efforts, ensuring they stay relevant, resonate with the audience, and drive desired business outcomes.

In conclusion, content marketing is a powerful tool that enables businesses to establish authority, create brand awareness, and engage their target audience. By developing a robust content marketing strategy, defining target audiences and content goals, and utilizing SEO best practices, businesses can craft compelling content, measure success through relevant KPIs, and make data-driven decisions to continually optimize their content marketing efforts.

7

Chapter 7: Maximizing Paid Advertising

Overview of paid advertising options

- Search engine advertising (Google Ads, Bing Ads)
  - Display advertising, social media ads, and native advertising

Creating effective ad campaigns

- Setting campaign objectives and budgets
- Targeting options and audience segmentation

Optimizing ad performance

- A/B testing and conversion rate optimization
- Retargeting strategies and ad frequency capping

Monitoring and analyzing ad campaigns

- Analyzing ad metrics and adjusting strategies accordingly
- ROI tracking and calculating advertising costs

Overview of Paid Advertising Options

Paid advertising has become an essential component of marketing strategies, allowing businesses to reach their target audience effectively and drive measurable results. In this overview, we will explore various paid advertising options, including search engine advertising, display advertising, social media ads, and native advertising. We will also delve into the key aspects of creating effective ad campaigns, such as setting objectives and budgets, targeting options, optimizing ad performance, retargeting strategies, and monitoring and analyzing ad campaigns.

Search Engine Advertising:

Search engine advertising involves displaying ads on search engine results pages (SERPs) when users search for specific keywords. The two major platforms for search engine advertising are Google Ads and Bing Ads. These platforms offer pay-per-click (PPC) advertising, where advertisers pay only when their ads are clicked. Search engine advertising enables businesses to reach potential customers actively searching for relevant products or services, increasing the likelihood of conversions.

Display Advertising, Social Media Ads, and Native Advertising:

Display advertising involves placing visual ads, such as banners or rich media, on third-party websites. These ads can appear in various formats, including images, videos, or interactive elements. Social media ads, on platforms like Facebook, Instagram, Twitter, and LinkedIn, leverage users' demographic, behavioral, and interest-based data to target specific audiences. Native advertising seamlessly integrates ads into the natural content flow of a website, making them appear less intrusive and more engaging.

Creating Effective Ad Campaigns:

To create effective ad campaigns, it is crucial to establish clear objectives and allocate appropriate budgets. Campaign objectives can vary, such as increasing brand awareness, driving website traffic, generating leads, or boosting sales. Setting realistic budgets helps ensure that ad campaigns can run smoothly and reach the desired audience consistently.

Targeting Options and Audience Segmentation:

Successful ad campaigns rely on accurate targeting and audience segmentation. Various targeting options are available, such as demographics (age, gender, location), interests, behaviors, and even specific keywords or websites. Audience segmentation allows advertisers to tailor their ads to specific customer segments, ensuring relevance and higher engagement.

Optimizing Ad Performance:

Optimizing ad performance involves continuous refinement to maximize the effectiveness of campaigns. A/B testing is a valuable technique where two versions of an ad are compared to determine which performs better. Conversion rate optimization focuses on improving the percentage of users who take desired actions, such as making a purchase or submitting a contact form.

Retargeting Strategies and Ad Frequency Capping:

Retargeting involves displaying ads to users who

have previously interacted with a brand's website or shown interest in its products or services. This strategy keeps the brand top-of-mind and encourages users to complete their intended actions. Ad frequency capping sets limits on the number of times an ad is shown to a particular user within a specific timeframe, preventing ad fatigue and ensuring a positive user experience.

Monitoring and Analyzing Ad Campaigns:

Regular monitoring and analysis of ad campaigns are crucial for assessing their performance and making data-driven decisions. Ad metrics, such as impressions, clicks, click-through rates (CTRs), conversions, and cost per acquisition (CPA), provide insights into campaign effectiveness. Analyzing these metrics helps identify areas for improvement and refine targeting strategies.

ROI Tracking and Calculating Advertising Costs:

Tracking return on investment (ROI) is essential to measure the profitability of ad campaigns. By comparing the revenue generated against the advertising costs, businesses can assess the campaign's success and make informed decisions regarding future investments. Calculating advertising costs involves considering the expenses associated with ad creation, platform fees, and ongoing optimization efforts.

In conclusion, paid advertising offers a range of options to reach and engage target audiences effectively. By leveraging platforms like search engine ads, display ads, social media ads, and native ads, businesses can create targeted campaigns to achieve specific objectives. Through careful planning, optimization, and analysis, advertisers can refine their strategies, track ROI, and achieve optimal results from their paid advertising efforts.

8

Chapter 8: Leveraging Influencer Marketing and Partnerships

U nderstanding influencer marketing and its benefits

- Identifying relevant influencers and brand ambassadors
- Developing mutually beneficial partnerships

Planning and executing influencer marketing campaigns

- Setting campaign goals and objectives
- Negotiating partnerships and collaborations

Maximizing influencer content and engagement

- Leveraging user-generated content (UGC)

- Encouraging audience participation and brand advocacy

Evaluating the success of influencer marketing

- Metrics for measuring influencer campaign performance
- Tracking ROI and adjusting strategies

Understanding Influencer Marketing and Its Benefits

In today's digital landscape, influencer marketing has emerged as a powerful strategy for brands to connect with their target audience and increase brand awareness. Influencers are individuals who have developed a loyal following and possess the ability to sway the opinions and behaviors of their followers. Leveraging the reach and influence of these individuals can be immensely beneficial for businesses. Here's a comprehensive guide to understanding influencer marketing and its benefits.

Identifying Relevant Influencers and Brand Ambassadors

The first step in influencer marketing is identifying relevant influencers and brand ambassadors who align with your brand's values, target audience, and niche. Conduct thorough research to find influencers who have a genuine connection with your industry and can effectively communicate your brand's message. Look for influencers with engaged followers and a track record of producing high-quality content.

Developing Mutually Beneficial Partnerships

Once you have identified potential influencers, it's crucial to develop mutually beneficial partnerships. Approach influencers with a clear value proposition and outline how collaborating with your brand can benefit them. It could be through monetary compensation, free products or services, exclusive access, or exposure to your brand's audience. Establishing a win-win situation is essential for nurturing long-term relationships.

Planning and Executing Influencer Marketing Campaigns

Planning and executing influencer marketing campaigns require a well-defined strategy. Set specific goals and objectives that align with your overall marketing objectives. Determine the campaign's target audience, messaging, desired outcomes, and key performance indicators (KPIs). Create a comprehensive campaign brief outlining the campaign's scope, deliverables, and timeline. Collaborate closely with influencers to ensure they understand your expectations and the campaign's desired outcomes.

Setting Campaign Goals and Objectives

To measure the success of your influencer marketing campaigns, it's crucial to set clear goals and objectives. These goals can vary depending on your brand's specific objectives, such as increasing brand awareness, driving website traffic, generating leads, or boosting sales. Ensure that your goals are specific, measurable, attainable, relevant, and time-bound (SMART) to track progress effectively.

Negotiating Partnerships and Collaborations

When engaging influencers, negotiation plays a vital role in securing successful partnerships. Negotiate terms that benefit both parties involved, such as the scope of work, compensation, exclusivity, and content usage rights. Maintain open communication and be flexible to reach a mutually beneficial agreement. Remember, a successful partnership is built on trust and shared value.

Maximizing Influencer Content and Engagement

Influencer content holds tremendous potential to resonate with your target audience. Encourage influencers to create engaging and authentic content that showcases your brand in a compelling way. Collaborate on content creation, ensuring that it aligns with your brand guidelines while allowing influencers creative freedom. Leverage the influencer's unique style and voice to maximize engagement and enhance the overall campaign impact.

Leveraging User-Generated Content (UGC)

User-generated content (UGC) is an invaluable resource for influencer marketing. Encourage your audience to create and share content related to your brand or campaign. UGC adds authenticity, expands your reach, and fosters a sense of community around your brand. Repurpose UGC across your marketing channels to further amplify its impact and build trust with your target audience.

Encouraging Audience Participation and Brand Advocacy

To cultivate a loyal community, encourage audience participation and brand advocacy. Create opportunities for your audience to engage with your brand and the influencers you collaborate with. Run contests, giveaways, and interactive campaigns that encourage user participation. Encourage influencers to actively engage with their audience, responding to comments, and fostering meaningful conversations around your brand.

Evaluating the Success of Influencer Marketing

Evaluating the success of influencer marketing campaigns requires comprehensive monitoring and analysis. Track key metrics such as reach, engagement, conversions, and sentiment analysis to assess the impact of your campaigns. Use analytics tools and social listening platforms to gain valuable insights into your campaign's performance and make data-driven decisions for future strategies.

Metrics for Measuring Influencer Campaign Performance

Metrics are essential for measuring the performance of your influencer campaigns. Key performance indicators (KPIs) to consider include follower growth, impressions, engagement rate, click-through rate (CTR), conversion rate, and return on investment

(ROI). Tailor your measurement strategy to align with your campaign objectives, and consistently monitor these metrics to evaluate the effectiveness of your influencer marketing efforts.

Tracking ROI and Adjusting Strategies

Tracking return on investment (ROI) is crucial to justify your influencer marketing spend. Analyze the revenue generated, cost per acquisition, and customer lifetime value to determine the monetary value generated by your campaigns. Continuously monitor ROI and be prepared to adjust your strategies based on performance insights. Iterate and optimize your approach to maximize the return on your influencer marketing investment.

In conclusion, influencer marketing is a powerful tool for brands to connect with their target audience, increase brand awareness, and drive conversions. By understanding the intricacies of influencer marketing, identifying relevant influencers, and developing mutually beneficial partnerships, brands can execute successful influencer marketing campaigns. Maximizing influencer content, leveraging user-generated content, encouraging audience participation, and evaluating campaign performance are essential steps to ensure the success of influencer marketing initiatives in the long run.

9

Conclusion

- Recap of key insights and strategies discussed in the book
- Encouraging readers to take action and implement the learned techniques
- Emphasizing the importance of continuous learning and adaptation in the ever-evolving digital marketing landscape
- Final words of advice and motivation from the author as a digital marketing expert with over 2 decades of experience

I **ntroduction**:
In the fast-paced world of digital marketing, staying ahead of the game is paramount. The book "Unleashing Digital Marketing Success" is a comprehensive guide that not only equips

readers with key insights and strategies but also motivates them to take action and adapt to the ever-evolving digital landscape. Authored by a seasoned digital marketing expert with over two decades of experience, this book serves as a compass for success in the dynamic realm of online marketing.

Recap of Key Insights and Strategies:
Throughout the book, readers have delved into a myriad of insightful concepts and practical strategies. The author expertly explains the importance of understanding one's target audience, emphasizing the power of personalized marketing. By segmenting audiences and crafting tailored messages, businesses can connect with their customers on a deeper level, forging lasting relationships.

The book also emphasizes the significance of data-driven decision making. Analyzing and interpreting data unlocks valuable insights into consumer behavior, enabling marketers to optimize their campaigns for maximum impact. By harnessing the power of analytics tools, businesses can identify trends, measure campaign performance, and refine their strategies to drive better results.

In addition, the author highlights the potential of social media as a powerful marketing tool. From building brand awareness to fostering engagement and loyalty, social media platforms offer an unprecedented opportunity to connect with audiences on a global scale. The book provides actionable tactics for leveraging different social media channels effectively, tailoring content to resonate with specific platforms and target demographics.

Encouragement for Implementation:
While knowledge is essential, taking action is where true transformation occurs. The book strongly encourages readers to implement the learned techniques, providing practical steps and case studies that illustrate their efficacy. By putting theory into practice, readers can begin their journey towards digital marketing success.

Emphasizing Continuous Learning and Adaptation:
The author fervently underscores the importance of continuous learning and adaptation in the ever-evolving digital marketing landscape. Technologies, algorithms, and consumer behaviors change rapidly, requiring marketers to remain agile and adaptable. By cultivating a mindset of continuous improvement and staying abreast of industry trends, professionals can stay ahead of the competition and seize new opportunities.

Final Words of Advice and Motivation:

As a digital marketing expert with over two decades of experience, the author leaves readers with words of wisdom and motivation. They remind us that success in digital marketing is not achieved overnight but is the result of persistence, resilience, and a commitment to excellence. They urge readers to embrace challenges as opportunities for growth and to keep pushing boundaries, as true breakthroughs often lie just beyond our comfort zones.

The author's final message is a call to action, urging readers to embark on their digital marketing journey with passion, purpose, and a hunger for knowledge. They emphasize that every successful campaign, every milestone reached, is a testament to the transformative power of digital marketing when combined with dedication and innovation.

Conclusion:

"Unleashing Digital Marketing Success" serves as a comprehensive roadmap for achieving success in the digital marketing realm. By recapitulating key insights and strategies, encouraging readers to take action, highlighting the importance of continuous learning, and providing final words of advice and motivation, the book equips marketers with the tools they need to navigate the ever-evolving digital landscape and unleash their full marketing potential.